Celebrations in My World

Mardi Gras and Carnival

Molly
Aloian

Crabtree Publishing Company

www.crabtreebooks.com

Crabtree Publishing Company
www.crabtreebooks.com

Author: Molly Aloian
Coordinating editor: Chester Fisher
Series and project editor: Penny Dowdy
Editor: Adrianna Morganelli
Proofreader: Crystal Sikkens
Editorial director: Kathy Middleton
Production coordinator: Katherine Berti
Prepress technician: Katherine Berti
Project manager: Kumar Kunal (Q2AMEDIA)
Art direction: Dibakar Acharjee (Q2AMEDIA)
Cover design: Tarang Saggar (Q2AMEDIA)
Design: Neha Kaul (Q2AMEDIA)
Photo research: Farheen Aadil (Q2AMEDIA)

Photographs:
Associated Press: p. 12
BigStockPhoto: stegodino: p. 9
The Bridgeman Art Library: Richard Hook/Private Collection/© Look and
    Learn: p. 10
Corbis: Vernon Bryant/Dallas Morning News: p. 28; Annie Engel/zefa: p. 7;
    Todd Gipstein: p. 18; Philip Gould: p. 17, 22; Blaine Harrington III:
    front cover; Stephanie Maze: p. 23; A.J. Sisco: p. 25; Joseph Sohm/
    Visions of America: p. 29; Nik Wheeler: p. 31
Dreamstime: Edward Mortimer: p. 21
Getty images: Garry Black: p. 30
Photolibrary: Index Stock Imagery: p. 19; Scott Payne: p. 5; Steve Vidler: p. 4
Reuters: Lee Celano: p. 14; Sean Gardner: p. 15, 27; Eduardo Munoz: p. 8, 26;
    Nikola Solic: p. 20
Shutterstock: Clara: p. 11; Perry Correll: folio, p. 24; GWImages: p. 13;
    Jan Kranendonk: p. 1; Bas Rabeling: p. 16; Sybille Yates: p. 6

Library and Archives Canada Cataloguing in Publication

Aloian, Molly
    Mardi Gras and Carnival / Molly Aloian.

(Celebrations in my world)
Includes index.
ISBN 978-0-7787-4755-0 (bound).--ISBN 978-0-7787-4773-4 (pbk.)

    1. Carnival--Juvenile literature. 2. Carnival--History--Juvenile
literature. I. Title. II. Series: Celebrations in my world

GT4180.A46 2010   j394.25   C2009-901923-X

Library of Congress Cataloging-in-Publication Data

Aloian, Molly.
    Mardi Gras and Carnival / Molly Aloian.
        p. cm. -- (Celebrations in my world)
    Includes index.
    ISBN 978-0-7787-4773-4 (pbk. : alk. paper) -- ISBN 978-0-7787-4755-0
(reinforced library binding : alk. paper)
    1. Carnival--Juvenile literature. I. Title. II. Series.

    GT4180.A46 2010
    394.25--dc22

                                                    2009013082

Crabtree Publishing Company
www.crabtreebooks.com   1-800-387-7650

Published in Canada
Crabtree Publishing
616 Welland Ave.
St. Catharines, ON
L2M 5V6

Published in the United States
Crabtree Publishing
PMB16A
350 Fifth Ave., Suite 3308
New York, NY 10118

Published in the United Kingdom
Crabtree Publishing
White Cross Mills
High Town, Lancaster
LA1 4XS

Published in Australia
Crabtree Publishing
386 Mt. Alexander Rd.
Ascot Vale (Melbourne)
VIC 3032

Contents

What is Mardi Gras?

Mardi Gras is a festive holiday. People dress up and throw parties. People have fun at the celebrations and parties. Mardi Gras falls on a different Tuesday between February 3 and March 9 every year.

People celebrate with parties, costumes, and parades.

DID YOU KNOW?

To find Mardi Gras, you must first find **Easter** Sunday on your calendar. From Easter, count 47 days backward. You have found Mardi Gras.

During Mardi Gras people eat delicious foods, such as this crawfish jambalaya.

Mardi Gras **traditions** began long ago during ancient winter festivals. Later, Christians saw it as a time to eat rich foods before **fasting**, or not eating, during **Lent**. Today, everybody joins in the fun.

Lent and Mardi Gras

Lent is a time when Christians give up something. It lasts for 40 days. Lent begins on Ash Wednesday and ends on Easter Sunday. Christians believe that Jesus is the Son of God and that he rose from the dead on Easter Sunday.

Jesus was **crucified**, or killed, on a cross on Good Friday.

DID YOU KNOW?

People celebrate Mardi Gras on the Tuesday before Lent. Long ago, Christians enjoyed the parties and food before Lent started.

People often eat pancakes the day before Lent begins.

Christians believe that Jesus gave up his life so that people's **sins** would be forgiven. They give up something during Lent to remember what Jesus gave up for them.

What is Carnival?

In Haiti, people celebrate this holiday as Carnival.

Mardi Gras has different names. Many people from around the world call this festive time Carnival. Carnival season begins on January 6 and lasts for weeks. The last day of Carnival is Mardi Gras.

DID YOU KNOW?

Mardi Gras means "Fat Tuesday" in French.

Some Carnival parties last for weeks.

Carnival means "good-bye to meat" in an ancient language. Long ago, people feasted on meat during winter festivals. They ate it all before it went bad.

Another name for Mardi Gras is Shrovetide. It begins three days before Lent. *Shrove* means "to have **confessed**, or told." Christians confess their sins during Shrovetide.

9

History of Mardi Gras

Long ago, people held winter festivals to make their gods happy. They believed these gods would bring spring and new crops to Earth.

In ancient times, people celebrated the winter festival Saturnalia.

DID YOU KNOW?

In the 1600s, many Europeans moved to North America. They brought their Mardi Gras traditions with them.

Long ago, people believed that Saturn brought spring and new crops to Earth.

Saturnalia was a winter festival held by ancient Romans. Saturnalia honored their god of **agriculture**, Saturn. People held parties and feasted. They chose a pretend king to rule over the festival. They wore masks and traded jobs for a day.

Mardi Gras Foods

Some people call Mardi Gras "Pancake Tuesday." Long ago, Christians cooked and ate pancakes to use up their eggs before Lent. Today, many still enjoy pancakes on this holiday.

Children take part in pancake-flipping races during Mardi Gras.

DID YOU KNOW?

On Pancake Tuesday people play pancake games that include pancake-flipping contests and races.

People also eat king cake for Mardi Gras. The tradition of a king cake dates back to Jesus' birth when three kings brought Him gifts. A plastic baby is baked inside the cake. The person who finds the baby in their cake must buy the king cake the next year.

King cakes are decorated in royal colors of gold, purple, and green.

Secret Clubs

People join secret Mardi Gras clubs to plan for parades and parties. In the United States, these secret clubs are called krewes. People in Brazil call them Samba schools. Every club has a special name.

The Krewe of Barkus members are dog-owners and their dogs.

DID YOU KNOW?

Children have their own club in New Orleans called the Krewe of Little Rascals!

The Krewe of Little Rascals
is a children's secret club.

Some clubs only allow members from the
same neighborhood. Others join together
because they are the same age, or have
the same interests. Together, the club
creates an idea for a parade **float**. Some
clubs prepare for Mardi Gras all year long.

Dressing Up

Part of the fun during Mardi Gras is pretending to be somebody different. People dress in colorful costumes and masks during Mardi Gras. Masks can be made of almost anything.

People dress in colorful costumes for Mardi Gras parades.

DID YOU KNOW?

When you wear a mask nobody knows it is you. During Mardi Gras, masked people visit friends to see if they can guess who they are.

Masks can be scary or funny.

Many masks are made from clay, feathers, straw, or beads. Groups of people in parades may wear costumes that look the same. Others dress up just for the fun of it. Some costumes are very beautiful. Others are scary or funny.

17

History of Carnival Parades

Mardi Gras parades began long ago during winter festivals. Actors dressed up as "winter" and "summer" during the 1400s in Europe. They paraded through the streets and pretended they were battling. Summer always won. This meant that warmer weather would soon come.

Some Carnivals in Europe are hundreds of years old.

One of the oldest Mardi Gras parades takes place during the Carnival of Venice. Wearing beautiful masks is an important part of this celebration.

Long ago, bulls were symbols to remind people to not eat meat during Lent.

DID YOU KNOW?

Hundreds of years ago in France, Christians paraded a bull through town on Mardi Gras to remind people not to eat meat during Lent.

19

Carnival Parades Today

Today, Mardi Gras parades are held in many different cities around the world. Groups of people design a moving platform called a float. Floats are built on top of a **vehicle**, or pulled by one.

People ring bells at the Rijeka Carnival parade.

DID YOU KNOW?

In Croatia, people ring bells during the Rijeka Carnival parade. This noisy tradition is supposed to scare winter away.

This huge float is part of a parade in Brazil.

Every float has a **theme**. Many are of giant figures, such as gods or heroes. Different **cultures** hold very different looking parades. Some of the largest parades are held in Brazil. Some floats are bigger than a two-story house!

21

Costume Balls

Mardi Gras is a time for dressing up and going to parties. Many secret clubs plan costume balls. A ball is a dance party. People dress up in fancy clothes. At a costume ball you can be a clown, a princess, or whatever you want to be.

People dress in fancy clothes or costumes for a costume ball.

DID YOU KNOW?

Not everyone can attend a costume ball for Mardi Gras. Special invitations are sent out, and only those invited can go.

People like to dance during
Mardi Gras parades, too.

When people have fun they like to dance.
Different cultures celebrate with different
dances. In Brazil, the official Carnival dance
is the samba. Quick-footed dancers swing
their hips and shoulders.

23

Royalty for a Day

Choosing a king for Carnival began during ancient winter festivals. Later, three kings brought baby Jesus gifts on **Twelfth Night**—held twelve days after Christmas. The following day, on January 6, Christians had a feast to celebrate **Epiphany**.

• People collect gold, green, and purple beads at Mardi Gras parties.

DID YOU KNOW?

Long ago in England, a bean was baked in the king cake. Whoever found the bean would be made king for the feast.

Kings are chosen for Mardi Gras parades and costume balls.

Secret clubs choose royalty every year for Carnival parades and balls. Purple, green, and gold are the official colors for Mardi Gras. They stand for justice, faith, and power.

25

Music of Carnival

Carnival music is fast and lively. It gets people singing, dancing, and having fun. Different cultures celebrate with different kinds of music.

In Haiti, musicians write songs especially for Carnival parades.

DID YOU KNOW?

"If Ever I Cease to Love," is the Mardi Gras theme song for New Orleans. It has silly words, like describing cows laying eggs.

In the United States, jazz music goes with Mardi Gras. New Orleans is the birthplace of jazz. In the Caribbean country of Haiti, musicians write songs especially for the Carnival season. Popular Haitian music for Carnival is *Zouk*. *Zouk* in English means "party."

Jazz music is popular for Mardi Gras in New Orleans.

Mardi Gras in New Orleans

The most famous Mardi Gras party in the United States is in New Orleans, Louisiana. Many businesses close. Children get the day off school. Families dress in costumes. They find a great place to see the parades and eat a picnic lunch together.

There is a lot for children to do during Mardi Gras.

DID YOU KNOW?

If you want to catch a souvenir from a Mardi Gras float, you have to shout "Throw me something, Mister!" when it passes by.

Mardi Gras is a chance to dress up and be whoever you want.

In New Orleans, Mardi Gras lasts for two weeks. Every day there are parades. Krewe members on floats toss throws, or souvenirs, out to parade-watchers. Throws are coins, necklaces, and stuffed animals.

29

Canada's Winter Carnival

It is cold in Canada during Carnival season. People enjoy the snow and ice at the Quebec Winter Carnival. Bonhomme—a snowman wearing a red hat and multi-colored belt—is the king of Carnival.

● Canada's Carnival King is a snowman called Bonhomme.

DID YOU KNOW?

Artists from all over the world compete at the Quebec Winter Carnival snow and ice sculpture competition.

At this Carnival you can watch boat races.
Some people even take snow baths in
their bathing suits. A new ice palace is
built every year for Bonhomme.

The ice bricks of the palace
line the walls that stand
over 66 feet (20 meters) tall.

Glossary

agriculture Crops and animals grown for food

confess To tell someone that you have done something wrong

culture The beliefs and customs of a group of people

Easter A Christian holiday that celebrates Jesus' return to life

Epiphany A Christian festival held on January 6 that celebrates the kings' visit to baby Jesus

fast To stop eating certain foods

float A moving display in a parade

Lent A 40-day period when Christians give up something

sculpture A form created by an artist

sin To break one of God's laws

theme A single subject or interest that remains the same

tradition A custom or belief handed down from one generation to another

Twelfth Night The evening of January 5 when the three kings visited baby Jesus

vehicle Something used to carry or move an object

Index

32

Printed in China—CT